For Better or Worse...

UNLESS ANNULMENT COMES FIRST

LEIGH ANNE W. HOOVER

For Better or Worse...Unless Annulment Comes First
Leigh Anne W. Hoover

Published November 2013
Little Creek Books
Imprint of Jan-Carol Publishing, Inc.
All rights reserved
Copyright © Leigh Anne W. Hoover

Wedding photography and front cover photograph by Overbay Photography.

Scripture taken from the HOLY BIBLE, NEW INTERNATIONAL VERSION Copyright © 1973, 1978, 1984 International Bible Society. Used by permission of Zondervan Bible Publishers.

In "God's Timing," excerpts from "Enjoying East Tennessee" columns first printed in *East Tennessee Medical News* reprinted with permission.

In "God in Dog," excerpts first appeared as a submitted "Letter to the Editor" in the *Kingsport Times-News.*

ISBN: 978-1-939289-54-4
Library of Congress Control Number: 2014958376

You may contact the publisher:
Jan-Carol Publishing, Inc
PO Box 701
Johnson City, TN 37605
publisher@jancarolpublishing.com
www.jancarolpublishing.com

Jan-Carol
Publishing, Inc
"every story needs a book."

Thank you, God, for my family and for blessing our lives.

*My husband, Brad, continues to inspire me every day,
and he remains the love of my life.*

Our adult son's strength and ongoing support of his sister has been unrivaled.

*This book is dedicated to my family, especially our daughter,
with much love and ongoing trust and faith in God's plan for our lives.*

Love,
Mama

Foreword

By Karen Spears Zacharias, author
Mother of Rain

As a former crime beat reporter, I have learned that the nicest, most respectable people can do the most unimaginable things. They will lie. They will cheat. They will swindle. And sometimes, too often really, they will murder those who get in their way. It is never easy to report on such cases. We don't want to face the truth when the truth involves changing our minds about someone we love.

I first heard the story you are about to read while attending a literary event at the lovely Allandale Mansion in Kingsport, Tennessee. The speaker that day was author Mary Alice Monroe. The first person to greet me as I stepped through the palatial doors of Allandale was the delightfully effervescent Leigh Anne Hoover.

Leigh Anne introduced herself and graciously welcomed me. Within a matter of minutes we discovered we had a lot in common. We were both writers, both friends of Mary Alice Monroe, and both had deep roots in local soil. We also had the added blessing of being mothers of daughters near the same age.

As Leigh Anne attended to matters of the event, I stood among the clipped hedges of the mansion's courtyard and visited with her daughter. As she related to me the details contained within the pages of *For Better or Worse...Unless Annulment Comes First*, I had two thoughts.

One was pure gap-mouthed unbelief. How could any man ever think of abandoning a woman as stunningly beautiful and as charmingly sweet as Leigh Anne's precious girl? I couldn't imagine it. I'll confess to thinking only an idiot would do something so foolish.

But then my second thought, one I expressed to both Leigh Anne and her daughter, was how fortunate she was that he chose to abandon her. I'd been a cop reporter long enough to know that murders often result because people who lead duplicitous lives are loathe to admit to their own deceitfulness. They would rather kill than admit to the truth of who they are. Rationale people can rarely understand that sort of behavior. Killing to protect a lie? But it happens every single day, all across this great nation of ours.

I remain thankful that Leigh Anne's daughter escaped such an ill-fated relationship.

For Better or Worse will stun you, it will leave you shaking your head, it will make you question how well you know the people you know, but ultimately, it will compel you to be more loving, more compassionate, more convinced than ever that knowing the truth and living the truth really does set a person free.

Acknowledgments

I cannot begin to express my most humble appreciation to the many people who have asked about our daughter, sent notes, cards and email messages and uplifted our family in prayers. From the ones who were in attendance at the wedding, to others sharing in our personal tragedy, your love and concern has been truly appreciated.

It has been absolutely amazing to watch this little book come together. Thanks are extended to publisher Janie Jessee for her willingness to share this story in a Christian book. I thank my editors Kasey Jones and Tammy Robinson Smith for always being on top of every detail and so quickly and graciously addressing each aspect along the way. Tara Sizemore, while on maternity leave, has done another exceptional job with the cover and each photo in the layout.

I have often heard there are no coincidences in life but many God-incidences. When our paths collide at just the right time, author Karen Spears Zacharias calls it "God's poetry."

I am most humbled by our "chance" meeting and the connections we share as writers and now friends. Karen's willingness to not only write the foreword but to also personally connect with my daughter and even navigate the details of the cover design for this book has all been an additional blessing. This could not have all been orchestrated without God.

Thank you to *New York Times* bestselling author Mary Alice Monroe for your endorsement, encouragement, interest and personal connection on so many levels. Just as you continue to capture the hearts of your readers, you are also endeared to my family. You remain my writing inspiration, mentor and a very special, treasured friend.

Finally, many thanks are extended to all of our cherished friends and family members for your ongoing love and prayers of support. God bless you.

Letter from the Author

Each of us is on a journey. Although none of us knows how long we have here on earth or how our lives will be used, God certainly does.

For our family, a wedding did happen. Amidst all of the love and emotion of any other wedding, it, too, included many, many blessings.

As Christians, we are not promised lives without adversities. In fact, I believe God uses these in our life journeys to mold us into His image.

When we accept Christ and ask Him to come into our lives, we are being molded to be more like Jesus. He has crafted every experience, including our joys and sorrows, and each will ultimately be used to His glory.

During our lives, we have the promise God is always with us through the Holy Spirit. Regardless of what we experience, God asks that we simply trust Him.

I believe God is using our family's wedding experience. Whether during the actual wedding or navigating the aftermath, God remains with us.

Through the Holy Spirit, He has given us the ability to share our trials to help and comfort others. In this faith sharing, we glorify Him, and that is my desire for this book. It is my prayer this little book will shine God's light and serve as a ministry to others.

Prologue

A Book?

John 9:3
*"'Neither this man nor his parents sinned,' said Jesus,
'but this happened so that the work of God might be displayed in his life.'"*

As I have gotten older, I have learned more about life experiences in relation to God, and many Bible studies have also helped me with this.

I've come to realize even though God does not cause adversities, but knowing they will make us stronger and ultimately be to His glory, He allows them. I also understand it is only by being transparent that we can share situations with others and offer hope through our own experiences.

We have free will. Regardless of our choices or situations, God is always with us. During adversity, God gives us strength, and He sends comfort through our friends and family. When we know the Holy Spirit is at work in our lives, and we are attuned to God, we desperately want to share this with others. Many refer to this as our testimony.

Life situations open our hearts, allowing us to empathize with others and to let them see the hope and love of Jesus here on earth through us. During our earthly lives, each of us is on a journey, and we are challenged to share His love with others.

I am a writer. Only through God can I exercise this gift, and if through writing, I can glorify Him, this adversity needs to be a book.

God is Always with Us

Esther 4:14

"For if you remain silent at this time, relief and deliverance for the Jews will arise from another place, but you and your father's family will perish. And who knows but that you have come to your royal position for such a time as this?"

In the midst of life's trials, it is common to feel aloneness. We often wonder if anyone else has ever felt our pain, loss and grief. This can be overbearing, and these feelings can also be very overwhelming.

Sometimes, we cannot possibly see beyond the next day, but we must remember to have faith and trust God. When no one else is with us, God is always beside us. Nothing in our lives is too big for Him to handle, and He has a plan for each of us.

We never truly know why one person endures an illness or a shattered dream, while another experiences a different burden or bears another cross. Yet, God knows, and He has a purpose.

Our choice is to rely on Him and trust in His timing to endure and get through situations. God uses adversities to give us strength and build character, to mold us into a reflection of His image.

Do not give up on your life. God is using everything for His ultimate plan. Reach out to Him for comfort, guidance and direction through prayer.

Every little girl dreams of her wedding and being a beautiful bride. What if the fantasy suddenly ended with the word "annulment"?

That is exactly what happened to our daughter, and my hope is that in sharing our story, others will be encouraged by evidences of God's enduring love.

Our daughter is a perfectionist, but we know perfection only exists in Christ. She followed the rules and has always tried to do the right thing. How could this have happened to her? And where was God?

As Christians, we are challenged to use our life stories to help others. We are able to do this because God is with us, and He resides in us through the Holy Spirit.

Although the outcome of the wedding was certainly not what we ever imagined, there were <u>many</u> blessings. We can see God at work throughout the wedding and the months that followed. My prayer is that I may use our story with this unfortunate situation to reflect His ultimate glory and give others abiding hope and comfort.

***

It was supposed to be one of the happiest times of our lives. Our only daughter was getting married during the Christmas holiday season in our church, her church. It had been a dream of hers since she was a little girl, and it was finally coming true.

Seasonal music and hymns filled the dimly lit sanctuary. The altar was adored with an arrangement of white roses, hydrangeas, cork-screw willow, magnolia and pine, all reverently honoring the cross. Alternating pews were marked by a glow from individual candles for the candlelight wedding service of celebration and blessing.

***

2 Corinthians 5:7
"For we live by faith, not by sight."

A radiant bride, she exuded pure joy and elegant, classic beauty. Just five years earlier, her heart had been broken when her engagement to her college sweetheart ended. The two had known each other since high school. The fact that he was an agonistic had never really posed a problem until it came time to meet with the hometown minister and begin premarital counseling, which typically precedes a Christian wedding.

During their dating years, she thought it was her duty as a Christian to convert him. Besides, it was not like he did not believe. He was just an intellectual, with a very scientific mind, and it was all about the essence of faith and believing in something that you cannot prove or even see. Yet because the very real power of the Holy Spirit is in us, as Christians, we know our God exists.

God always works things to His ultimate good, and not being properly yoked can cause problems in a marriage—especially years later when children are involved.

She had planted the seed and watered it with prayers. Ultimately, it would be up to him to accept Christ as his Savior and to grow and nurture his faith. At least he was able to sever the engagement and let her go.

Once the engagement to her college sweetheart ended, she returned home to Kingsport, Tennessee. In fact, the day we received the frantic phone call, we met her on the highway. Her father told her to drive as far as she could from Memphis, knowing we were driving from Kingsport, which is located at the tip of Tennessee, right at the Virginia state line.

She had been in Memphis looking for a teaching job because her fiancé was planning to enter medical school. Once married, this was where they would be living, and she needed a job.

Not knowing where we would meet, our cars set out to find each other on the interstate. Hers was loaded with unbridled emotions and all of her possessions, and ours was filled with angst and anticipation.

Of course, we stayed in contact through cell phones, and when our cars finally met somewhere in middle Tennessee, she sprang from her vehicle like a jack-in-a-box and collapsed in our arms, both mentally and physically exhausted.

Weeks went by, and the two did not talk. It had ended.

Frustrated, she would spend hours in bed replaying the scenario and reliving every detail. One day, I finally declared it was officially time to move on with her life. I challenged her to think about where she wanted to live and teach. If necessary, she needed to start trying to relocate.

Teaching jobs are difficult to find—especially in a good district—but she landed an available interim position in Greenville, South Carolina, and she temporarily moved in with some friends from college.

Between moving to a new city, starting a new job and fending off every ailment a kindergartner could possibly have, the adjustment about killed her. It was also very taxing on the friendships.

As the year progressed, and she settled into a routine, the next step was finding a more permanent residence. Once again, she moved into an apartment with a girlfriend, but this time, she did have her own room.

Rent rivaled the cost of a small house payment. Once she secured a teaching position for the following year, she decided to actually look for a home. We never envisioned she would meet her future husband through her realtor, but that is exactly what happened.

Moving On

Eventually, hearts heal, and so did hers. With a fresh start in new city and her first job as an elementary school teacher, she had moved on in life.

Although she was in another state, the city was very close to her alma mater, which was a nearby college town. This made going back for tailgating and football games fun and easy.

The transition also meant a new home, and hers was conveniently located within walking distance of downtown and just minutes from her school. Ironically, the recommended realtor also just happened to have a brother.

Although guarded and reluctant to let another into her heart, love did emerge, and it grew. He was quite a bit older, nine years to be exact.

The age difference concerned her because she did not know how we, her parents, would feel about it. If you are that much older and have never been married, is there a reason? This should have been the first red flag.

He had grown up in a small town. His mother was a teacher, and his father spent a career on the road, which left the childrearing responsibilities to the mother. Although she did the very best she could under the circumstances, there was not a lot of masculine influence for her son.

He did all of the expected "boy type" activities, but not having a masculine role model left him like Jacob from the Bible.

Like Jacob, he was able to cook and learned some domestic skills, but his mother also doted on him. As an older parent, his mother was from a generation where this was expected. She did everything for her children and believed this was the best example.

Unfortunately, most who receive this type of upbringing believe they are entitled in life and look for a mate who will provide and fill this role as caregiver.

He developed a caring heart, but he harbored resentment for not being shown other, manly activities or having a masculine role model.

When they began dating, she knew this about him, but what originally attracted her was the caring side of this man. He would listen to endless conversations about her classroom and school activities.

Her father is a gifted listener, but she had heard this was not always the norm for men. It's often said that a girl will look for someone like her father to marry. To this day, I believe this shared, caring heart and listening trait is what attracted her to him.

The men in our family are caring, but they are also hunters and more like Jacob's brother, Esau. In fact, the first time she brought him home, her brother had just shot a deer with his bow and planned to clean it later in the evening at a friend's farm.

Of course, he was invited to go, too, but like Jacob, he was not interested in the outdoors. He was definitely not a hunter/gatherer type of man.

Annulment

1 Corinthians 7:15
"But if the unbeliever leaves, let him do so.
A believing man or woman is not bound in such circumstances;
God has called us to live in peace."

Where the strong and stately steeple once stood among those of other denominations surrounding historic Church Circle in Kingsport, Tennessee, the one from First Broad Street United Methodist, our church, had been removed for much needed repairs. It was not expected to be restored before the wedding.

Shrouded in a blue tarp, the image was an eyesore to our daughter. Of course, we reassured her that no one would even notice the missing steeple on the church. It would be dark, and Church Circle would be alive with holiday lights, the Christmas tree and nativity scene. No one would even look up in the dark night to the sky. In hindsight, it was replete with symbolism for the impending, doomed marital union.

As the ladies gathered in the parlor prior to the wedding, the men were also together. The groom was noticeably quiet. Yet, it seemed in keeping with his personality to be somewhat nervous. This was a major life decision, and these always seemed to make him second-guess himself.

In a front row seat during the ceremony, I did not notice his "deer in the headlights" expression that others described later. Again, I am not sure this would have been alarming because he never appears confident.

During the vows, there was a noticeable pause. Our daughter looked at her bridegroom, signaling it was his turn to repeat the vows.

As they exchanged wedding rings, he extended his right hand versus his left. He said this was because he was nervous and that he had not done this intentionally. Yet, later he commented it might mean they were not really married.

***

The following morning, family members gathered in our house. We had plenty of food left over from the wedding reception, and all were invited over to enjoy it before heading home to their respective states.

The wonderful thing about weddings is family being together for a happy occasion. In large families, such as ours, unfortunately as children get older and lives get busier, this becomes more and more difficult.

However, because the wedding was over the holidays, cousins were out on school and college breaks, so schedules were more easily adjusted for all to attend.

Plus, since she is a teacher, it was great for the bride. She had a few more days off for a honeymoon, and everything was still beautifully decorated for the holidays.

Of course, the newlyweds also joined us for this gathering and lively discussion about the festivities from the night before. We even had a copy of the wedding announcement and bridal portrait from the Sunday morning newspaper, as it was customary to publish the photo the day after the wedding—especially in the South.

Although somewhat reticent, he did look at the article, her portrait on the wall in the dining room and joined in on the conversation. However, he also disappeared to sit alone in the den.

This, too, did not alarm me because I was sure he, too, must have been both mentally and physically exhausted. It's very tiring to engage and talk with so many well-wishers, and the after party had gone into the wee hours.

As others left, and we were there with our daughter and her new husband, it was concerning that he did not want the "Just Married" sign added to their getaway vehicle. She was excited and briefly pleaded for this, yet she resigned when he seemed adamant about not wanting to display it.

Accepting the Situation

Romans 15:13
*"May the God of hope fill you with all joy and peace as you trust in him,
so that you may overflow with hope by the power of the Holy Spirit."*

As with any tragedy, there are many emotions, and each person involved or even touched handles the situation with his or her own, individual response.

Like death, there are stages of grief. Once you deal with the initial shock of the incident, you move through the processes, which include stages of healing.

Personally, I have a true peace. I deeply regret our daughter is hurting, but I know and trust God and His plan.

Why did the wedding have to happen? Many have asked this question, but I do not believe there was any other way.

If her father and I had not accepted him and refused to let her marry, she would have always questioned if he was the love of her life. Ultimately, she would have also resented us for keeping her from this person and still would have tried to see him. This could have gone on indefinitely, and it would have torn us all apart.

Although the fact that the groom mentioned annulment on the new bride's honeymoon is nearly unfathomable, it was a blessing.

In his heart, he knew he could not be the type of husband she needed. He professed love, but it was not the level of love God has reserved for a husband and wife.

In essence, although the realization may seem untimely, and even too late, he did everyone a favor by giving up the charade early.

The peace I have now is only possible through the Holy Spirit.

Weddings

1 Corinthians 13: 4-8, 13

*"Love is patient, love is kind. It does not envy, it does not boast, it is not proud.
It is not rude, it is not self-seeking, it is not easily angered, it keeps no record of
wrongs. Love does not delight in evil but rejoices with the truth. It always protects,
always trusts, always hopes, always perseveres. Love never fails."*
"And now these three remain: faith, hope and love. But the greatest of these is love."

As friends and family gathered for the celebration and blessing of marriage, an entire passage of scripture, 1 Corinthians 13: 1-13, was read from the pulpit. Both longtime and newly married couples held hands and listened to these words of promise.

Regardless of the outcome, which occurred less than 48 hours later, there was a wedding, and she was a bride. In his wake, the marriage is annulled, which means it never happened, but it did.

All of the joy, love and attention that goes into any traditional wedding was involved in hers. Yet, when the pictures arrived, and the video was finished, there was no celebration.

Her bridal portrait still hangs in the dining room, and memories of the day it was taken flood over my heart. There was so much excitement and anticipation leading her into the next stage of her life.

Their wedding invitation, with her beautiful, full family name, is in the china cabinet along with our wedding invitation and her grandparents', my mama and daddy's. It's difficult.

Only after the wedding can most people truly enjoy and take in all that transpired after the many months of planning.

Regardless of the outcome, the experience was real. The wedding was in our church, and a covenant was made at the altar before God.

Unfortunately, a promise can only be kept if both parties are willing to guard, protect and uphold the covenant. She tried. Oh, she tried. But his heart was elsewhere, and this is why we did not know of her suffering for weeks.

She had taken a vow, and the words were sacred. When she proclaimed, "For better or for worse...," surely, this was the worst.

He was scared and still frightened about all of the expectations that came with being a "husband." She knew him and reassured him in his doubt.

Months later, we learned of these ongoing words of reassurance. "It's OK. I am here," were even expressed by our daughter at the altar. She is strong.

Well-meaning young women encouraged her to hold fast. Yet, when your husband lets go, there is nothing to hold on to.

In his mind, he probably felt all consumed. As the wedding approached, he was overwhelmed and nearly drowning, while trying to be someone he is not.

However, he still professed his love for our daughter, so it seemed in character with his other, major life decisions. This man was just different, and he was used to others making decisions for him. Apparently, they had also made this one and told him to marry our daughter. So, he did.

Knowing this makes the anger subside some for me. He was not able to take a stand and felt no one was listening. In asking for an annulment on their honeymoon, he must have finally felt "in control."

Would there have ever been a good time for this? No, there probably would not have been. One day, we may know and see things more clearly.

17

In fact, I believe the wedding had to happen, or our daughter would have always wondered about this man. She loved him, and he said he loved her. Again, if we had insisted they not marry, she would have blamed us. If she had given in to his ongoing indecisiveness, they would still be engaged. He cannot make decisions for himself.

By finally having the courage to stand up, albeit very late, his request for an annulment was actually an admittance of failure, and it was his only perceived way out of the relationship. It did not have to be like this, but, as one friend said, apparently, "He was drowning, and this was his only way to keep his head above water."

It did not have to be this way. Yet, he thought it did, and maybe that was because of her history with a broken engagement.

Maybe he just wanted her to have her wedding. But, it should have been with the right groom. A quote made by Anna in the infamous Public Broadcasting Service masterpiece drama *Downton Abbey* comes to mind.

"I'd rather have the right man, than the right wedding." — Anna, S2E5

Did he not know this? No matter how difficult, or how much it would have hurt, to go through with the wedding of her dreams with the wrong man was not right.

I have often told our daughter, "Anyone can be a bride."

Too often, girls get wrapped up in the festivities and all of the attention. She was not like this and truly felt her groom had arrived because she also loved his family—especially his mother.

Her Southern background and mannerisms were compared to those of her own grandmother, my late mother. The two became friends, and I do believe his mother loved our daughter. Maybe this is why he could not call off the wedding.

Ultimately, he did not want to break his own mother's heart or upset his aging grandmother, who was her mother. In the end, I do believe, he hurt both.

Other Weddings

Of course, other friends were engaged, and many, many weddings would follow. During those required parties, our daughter was not shunned, but it was as if she never even had a wedding. She had, and her wedding was what she had always wanted.

Her father and I trusted her decision to marry, and we accepted this man based on her love and his commitment to loving her. Of course, we went forward with the wedding she had always wanted. She's our only daughter, and this was her big day.

However, "well-meaning" people often implied that she knew nothing about being married because her marriage was annulled, which means it never happened. But, it did.

Our daughter would say, "I may not have been a wife, and I may not have a marriage, but I was definitely a bride, and I did have a wedding."

Engagements

Our daughter was so serious about commitment that she often expressed her displeasure with premarital counseling. In her mind, it is offered too late. To her, it makes more sense to have pre-engagement counseling with clergy because once the engagement happens, everything is compounded.

After an engagement ring has been given, everyone knows about the impending marriage, and the planning begins. Why would couples, serious about wanting to become engaged, not seek counseling prior to this step?

Of course this interferes with the element of surprise, but is the long-term importance and commitment not worth more than an over-done surprise?

She gave her heart to a man who had also asked her father for her hand in marriage. They had done the right things, and she loved him.

God's Timing

Jeremiah 29:11
"'For I know the plans I have for you,' declares the LORD,
'plans to prosper you and not to harm you, plans to give you hope and a future.'"

When we turn everything over to God, we realize that His timing is <u>always</u> perfect. Because God knows how to complete each and every life puzzle, He knows when and where each piece is needed. All of the little pieces have to come together in just the right way to form our life picture.

Several years ago, my husband happened upon an auction for a property, which has become a second home on Daufuskie Island, South Carolina. At the time, I could not imagine how this barrier island, which has no bridge, would even remotely be of interest. I was wrong.

The island is a tiny piece of paradise for the Hoover side of the family, and it has already become a treasured getaway.

Once a thriving oyster community, the Gullah, which were freed African-American slaves, made up the population. Many worked in what became a world-renowned, leading commodity for the five-mile, Lowcountry Sea Island off the coast of South Carolina. However, in 1959, once fertile beds were deemed polluted by neighboring industry. With the harvest no longer safe, most were forced off the island to seek employment.

There is still no bridge to the mainland. However, a short ride on a ferry, water taxi, or personal boat from Savannah, Georgia, Bluffton or Hilton Head Island, South Carolina (where you will also likely see a dolphin or two) can truly take visitors back in time to the dusty roads of Daufuskie.

Tourists will discover an island steeped in history and listed on the National Register of Historic Places. Whether you're part of a scheduled tour with a colorful guide or exploring in your own golf cart, it is a daytrip worth the adventure!

From the deviled crab makers (only three remain on the island, and you can buy them frozen directly from their homes) to a potter at the Silver Dew Pottery, a talented sculptor at the Iron Fish, the t-shirt lady and others, artisans and craftsmen abound on Daufuskie. Each has a talent or two, and each is definitely an interesting character.

Many recall Daufuskie Island from author Pat Conroy's book *The Water is Wide*. Conroy spent a year on the island he refers to as "Yamacraw" in the novel while an elementary school teacher at Mary Fields School. The book is a memoir of his experience. The school was built in 1930, and community meetings are still held there today.

The Daufuskie Island Historical Foundation was founded in 2001, and the organization has done a remarkable job with preserving much of the island's historical sites. There is also a museum and Gullah Learning Center where visitors can learn all about their culture.

Only main roads on the island are paved, so the predominant mode of transportation is via golf cart. With just four island restaurants, for an extended stay, visitors have to plan out their menus and bring groceries over to the island. Small sacrifices, or rather, thoughtful planning, allow one to reap the reward of a natural island and a private retreat.

I would have never imagined how much my family would connect to the island, but God knew. From our Labrador retrievers enjoying frolics on the private beaches and rides in the golf carts, to our son,

Bradley, working as the managing director and lead guide of Tour Daufuskie and currently living on the island fulltime, I would have never envisioned these pieces of our life puzzle.

In fact, Daufuskie even played a role in the wedding. Our daughter's bachelorette weekend was held on the island over her fourth of July birthday weekend, and her bridegroom later took the groomsmen there for a bachelor weekend, too.

In coordinating colors, my mother-in-law embroidered each bridesmaid's monogram, as well as "Daufuskie Island," on special towels. Her friends even had koozies made with "Daufuskie" emblazoned on them.

Memories of this, as well as other shared times on the island, are detailed in the villa's journal. Are the pages still there? Of course, they are. Despite the outcome of the wedding, these musings are memories.

The last time we visited, one of the towel favors tumbled down from the stored pile of other beach towels. Seeing it made me smile, and on that day, I took that very towel to the beach.

***

As a journalist, I write a monthly column, which is entitled "Enjoying East Tennessee," in *East Tennessee Medical News*. After discovering Daufuskie and learning so much about the island, I began writing about it. My January column in the publication is always a "departure" feature, and for the past three years, it has been on Daufuskie Island.

A metal fish sculpture hangs on our screened-in back porch. The special fish is reminiscent of days on Daufuskie Island, and its hidden signature eye reminds me of the wonderful artist Chase Allen.

The year I featured Chase Allen of the Iron Fish Gallery in my column, I was most impressed with this young man's morals and values. Handsome, with a gorgeous smile, Allen looks like he stepped right out of a novel by Nicholas Sparks. And, the fact that he creates his art from one of the few remaining Gullah oyster shanties on the island makes him even more intriguing.

During October 2012, I was on the island for the second annual Literacy Throwdown and the release of resident author Roger Pickney's new novel. My little children's books were proudly displayed alongside those of visiting *New York Times* bestselling authors Dorthea Benton Frank, Mary Alice Monroe and Patti Callahan Henry. As I sat beside my friend Mary Alice, and met the other literary ladies, I was honored to be in the presence of such legends and talent on Daufuskie Island.

When I met Mary Alice's friend and fellow bestselling author, Patti Callahan Henry, I learned more about her connection to Daufuskie, an island she refers to as "Oystertip" Island in her novels. Additionally, I discovered that she also knows, loves and admires Chase Allen's work.

In fact, the *New York Times* bestselling author was actually one of Allen's first fish customers. Daufuskie Island is a creative muse for many, and talents abound on the island. So, while I was there, I sat down one-on-one with the young artist and creator of my special fish.

Artistry was in his genes, yet up until a little over 10 years ago, Allen had never truly pursued it. With a degree in marketing from the University of North Carolina Wilmington, following college, Allen was hired by International Paper and actually worked as an intern in the marketing department on the Haig Point side of the island, which was followed by a brief stint as a real estate agent where he worked exclusively for a developer. However, he was miserable, and this was not the ideal profession for an admitted outdoorsman.

A fan of fishing, the water, marshes and the seasons, Allen loved the island and always escaped to the historical side whenever he could. Following September 11, 2001, several things also happened in Allen's own life, and he decided our "tomorrows" are never guaranteed. This enlightened viewpoint was the push Allen needed to pursue another avenue and to live his dream.

Allen enrolled in technical course in Savannah, and with his talent, he produced a metal pig for the island school auction. After that, he was hooked. Shortly after, the September 11th disaster occurred, the real estate company left for Florida. However, Allen had no desire to go. And with that, his new career was born.

He cut all ties with real estate and even let his license expire. Allen ultimately accredits the knowledge and recognition of his need for a career change to divine intervention, everything correctly lining up and to taking the ultimate "leap of faith."

Today, customers continually find his gallery either in person, down a dusty Daufuskie road on the historic side of the island, or online, and they remind Allen of how blessed he truly is to be doing what he enjoys and earning a living. His unique metal and artwork hangs in residences, offices and restaurants across the country and internationally, and his work has been featured in publications including *Coastal Living, Southern Living, Deep Magazine, Hilton Head Monthly* and others.

The Iron Fish Gallery body of work includes everything from yard sculptures to huge fish, mermaids, blue crabs and stingrays. His most recent creations are actually framed pieces with additional cutouts for enhanced lighting.

Allen operates out of his home and backyard workshop. His home, which is one of the few available island Gullah shanty homes, he fixed up himself. In fact, island visitors can purchase their art selections directly off the porch on the honor system and slide their payment under his front door.

During our interview, I kept thinking our son would love to meet Allen, and I told him. Of course, the timing was not right yet because Bradley needed to finish school and graduate from Clemson.

Little did I know, but Allen had been germinating the idea of an island outdoor tour company. In fact, the concept had been in the works for seven years, but he did not have the needed person he could trust to run it.

Immediately following his last semester at Clemson, Bradley attended Georgia Outdoor College and became certified as a Wilderness First Responder. This led to additional certifications in outdoor leadership and volunteer opportunities with the Southeastern Wilderness Medicine conference, which was founded by Dr. Chris Moore.

I had interviewed Dr. Moore for a variety of articles and knew Bradley would also enjoy working with him. In addition to heading up wilderness medicine, Moore is also an avid outdoorsman, and he wrestled in college. Bradley was on the Clemson University club wrestling team.

Following graduation in August, Bradley moved to Greenville, South Carolina, and he began working with an established company. However, shortly after the holidays, the company made several layoffs, and his job was the first to go.

When my phone rang at lunchtime, I answered, only to hear the sound of my 23 year-old-son's voice crack with the news he had lost his job, and he had not done anything wrong. Timing....

Bradley was in Greenville for a reason, and God knew exactly where he needed to be at that time. His sister was also there, and when she was not teaching, she was writing wedding thank you notes and trying to create a new home with her husband.

Unfortunately, her husband was traveling a lot with his job or staying at his office and was never there. As newlyweds, this should have been a time of newfound joy and happiness, yet it was quite the opposite. When he was home, there was a lot of friction and hostility in the relationship.

Her brother was available for odd jobs, such as painting bathrooms, and he helped her. While there, the two talked, and Bradley began to realize something was not right.

On Valentine's Day, we stopped for an overnight stay in Greenville on our way to Daufuskie. We stayed in Bradley's apartment and offered to meet and talk with the newlyweds. We have always been willing and available to listen and wanted to help if we could. However, he did not think it was a good idea without his own parents being there, too.

That night, he stayed in a hotel. We made arrangements to cut our trip short and come back to Greenville in time to meet with his family on Monday.

In the meantime, Bradley went to Daufuskie with us, and it was on this trip that his destiny would take a turn.

***

We were only on the island for a few short days. It's never long enough, and every time we go to Daufuskie, we always discover something new.

One of the things I always try to do is go by the Iron Fish. If he's home, it's a treat to catch-up with Chase Allen and his wife, Rachel, who teaches Spanish on Hilton Head Island.

Recently unemployed, Bradley felt like a third wheel, but I encouraged him to come. If the Allens were home, I knew he would enjoy seeing Chase again. The two had actually met on a number of island visits, and Bradley has always been fascinated with his work. However, he didn't know just how important this meeting would be, but God sure did.

As expected, Allen was home on this particular afternoon in February, and we enjoyed catching-up with the young artist. He and Bradley also engaged in a conversation about a plan Allen had been developing for about seven years.

Being an avid outdoorsman, Allen was searching for someone to help with an island excursion adventure business. He knew the natural beauty of the island is unrivaled, and from kayaks and paddle boards, to bikes and canoes, people enjoy exploring it.

However, Allen needed the right person for the business to work and someone he could trust as a friend and colleague. He found his man in our son, and Tour Daufuskie, LLC opened on April 7, 2014.

God Knows

Philippians 4: 6-7
"Do not be anxious about anything, but in everything,
by prayer and petition, with thanksgiving, present your requests to God.
And the peace of God, which transcends all understanding,
will guard your hearts and your minds in Christ Jesus."

People come into our lives for different reasons. I once read something comparing life to a train ride and mentioning that each of us is on a journey. Some will be with us for a while, and others will come and go as their stops happen. Each has a purpose.

The first time I experienced a job loss was after I had been with a company for nearly 17 years. It had been my first job after college graduation, and my coworkers were like family.

During these years, my mother was battling breast cancer that spread to her bones. As Christians we are told to trust God and not to worry, yet as a young woman, I worried and was concerned how I would be able to leave my job to be with her when the time came.

Surprisingly, right before Christmas in 1999, the sales division of the television station was being sold to another affiliate. Members of our team were offered contracts to go to another station in a neighboring town, and we had to decide that day if we would accept.

31

Our group was gathered off premise to make the decision. I was able to locate my husband, Brad, and he was allowed to review my contract at the site. Nothing in me made me want to leave and join this new venture. I did not know why or what I would do, but I knew I did not need to sign the contract. Together, we made the decision not to opt for this, and that ended my career in television advertising sales.

However, this freed me to begin writing more and afforded me the opportunity to work out of our home as an independent contractor. Most importantly, this newfound freedom allowed me to be with our children during their formative high school years. Ultimately, it also provided the freedom that I needed to be with my mother.

Always driven, Mama's passion was for her husband, children, grandchildren and anything that had to do with beautification. She was a former president of the Garden Club of South Carolina, South Atlantic Regional Director for the National Garden Club, landscape critic, master flower show judge, master gardener and the list continues; beautification was Mama's gift. Everything she touched through her service in the state of South Carolina and elsewhere was simply magnificent. In fact, the governor even awarded her the Order of the Palmetto, which is the state's highest civilian honor.

Prior to Mama's passing, I remember explaining her gift to a journalist during an interview.

"If there's a garden club in heaven, she will be in it," I explained. "If not, she will organize one and make us all join!"

Throughout years of cancer treatments, she continued her efforts with gardening and beautification. Despite her pain, she remained involved and interested in others.

I remember going to an in-depth garden and study club meeting with her. Since I was unemployed, or at least working in a different fashion than usual, I could go home for more weekday, special events. This particular meeting was being held in the home of a gardener who grew and sold daylilies.

I was able to attend, hear the lesson about lilies and even purchase some for our yard in Tennessee.

During the informative lecture, Mama casually excused herself from the room. Concerned, I, too, slipped out and followed only to find her in the bathroom nauseated from the chemotherapy. As I patted her back and got something cool for her face, I realized the frailty this tiny woman usually masked.

Undeterred in spite of this, we rejoined the group as if nothing happened and made our way outside to make our own daylily selections. It was such fun, and we found varieties in just the right color for my home.

Weeks later, we laughed because one of the more expensive varieties that she had selected had accidentally been transferred to my car. However, since Brad had already planted it, I declared she wasn't getting it back!

Mama's knowledge about flower gardening was always so impressive to me, but she causally shared it with us, and we ended up learning more than we ever imagined.

In fact, as a grown woman, I was visiting the Festival of Flowers at our church, First Broad Street United Methodist Church in Kingsport, Tennessee, with a dear friend. The two of us were admiring some of the arrangements, and I commented on the digitalis in one of them.

Immediately, my sweet and well-meaning friend said, "Oh, that's foxglove."

Perplexed, I agreed but remained convinced it looked exactly like digitalis!

Of course, I would later learn foxglove and digitalis are one in the same. Mama always made sure we learned the botanical names, and, of course, the botanical name for foxglove is digitalis!

Mama would always say that gardening made her feel close to God. I am sure when she was in her famed flowerbeds, she would thank God for her many blessings and for the beauty of His earth.

I still have one of her favorite Bible verses penned in her handwriting in my own Bible.

Philippians 4:13 *"I can do everything through him who gives me strength."*

That summer, in August 2003, I was at home in South Carolina visiting my parents. Mama had lived for 15 years with breast cancer, which had metastasized to her bones. She had always been a small, petite woman, but now, at under 100 pounds, she was like a little bird.

Of course, she maintained a full calendar and kept going. A voracious reader, she was checking out more and more books from the library and having to put a "pencil check" in the back corner to remember those she had read.

One evening, she called me into her room. Lying on her bed, this frame of a woman held my hand and asked that I feel a hardened knot in her abdomen.

Concerned, I mumbled, "Oh, Mama. Have you asked your oncologist about this?"

"It's probably nothing," she replied. "But, I have an appointment and will show him."

We knew it could not be good, but my brother, who had graduated from West Point and had a career in the army, was due home from a deployment, and she had planned his favorite meal. In fact, we had already been to the grocery store and the farmer's market to get most of the items. This dinner never happened.

Daddy did not understand why, after visiting her oncologist, she was immediately hospitalized. Joe was coming home, and she had special plans. I explained this was serious and exactly why she needed to be admitted.

This otherwise stoic woman, knowing her child was coming home from war, had even agreed. She knew....

It was cancer—endometrial and uterine. A hysterectomy revealed that the cancer had spread throughout her body. Joe did arrive home, and our mother was radiant the night he entered her hospital room.

Glowing like an angel in her bed jacket, an item saved for occasions when one might have to be in the hospital, I have never seen our mother more radiant. Throughout those weeks of anguish, she had masked her pain waiting for her son to come home.

God's timing is always perfect. I had been freed of a job commitment, which enabled me to spend much-needed time in South Carolina. My middle brother was home and on extended leave, and my other two brothers were also there to care for our mother, who had given so much of herself to us.

Eventually, we would end all tests and medical procedures, opting instead to bring her home to their sunroom, which became her bedroom.

Each of our spouses and our collective children, her 10 grandchildren, had all rotated in and out during this window. However, on what would become her final night, just Daddy, my three brothers and I were there together.

As always, His timing was perfect. Everything was orchestrated to happen according to His will.

At sunrise, my youngest brother, Chris, awakened me and my brother Joe, who was in the downstairs bedroom. Chris had already called Trip, and he was on his way from his house in town. We gathered in the sunroom with our father by her bedside, and we each said our goodbyes to our dear mother.

I reassured her that we had found her notes about favorite hymns and scripture and told her about our plans for her service. We assured her it was fine to leave us to be with God in heaven. We thanked her for being such a wonderful woman and for loving us all so very much. We told her Daddy would be fine.

When Trip came through the door, she knew her family was gathered. As the white viburnum, just outside the sunroom windows, miraculously bloomed a second time in the courtyard, a tear rolled down her cheek. Together, we surrounded her bedside, prayed, whispered "I love yous," and she peacefully went to sleep.

Tradition

Isaiah 41:10
*"So do not fear, for I am with you; do not be dismayed,
for I am your God. I will strengthen you and help you;
I will uphold you with my righteous right hand."*

In 1984, the first year we were married, a decorative Christmas plate arrived in the mail from the Bradford Exchange. It was a gift from my husband. Since then, he has continued to ensure the holiday plate's arrival each summer, and I have loved collecting the special plates.

The first couple of years we were married, the Norman Rockwell paintings pictured a Santa on the *Rockwell Christmas* annual plates. Then in 1986, Santa appeared with a sleeping, little girl. Ironically, that was the year our daughter was born.

The series returned to Santa until 1990. That year, Santa was not on the plate. Rather, a little boy kneeling in prayer beside his bed graced the plate. That same year, after enduring surgery for secondary infertility, our son was born. It was an answered prayer, indeed.

When the Christmas plate arrived during our daughter's engagement in the summer of 2013, preceding the holiday wedding, the title, "On Thin Ice!," should have been a warning. Instead of the normal picturesque scene, the 2013 plate depicted an unsteady

young boy on ice-skates ready to fall at any moment. Others were laughing and running away. Even the dog was exiting the scene!

***

It has always been important to our daughter that she be married in church. It could not be just any church; she wanted to be married in our church in her hometown. To say we are a traditional family, and she was a traditional bride, would be an understatement.

I did not have to impose any of my desires on this young woman. We liked the same things about a wedding, and it was my delight to plan it for her.

In fact, back in 1983, after becoming engaged to my college sweetheart, Mama did the very same thing for me. We were going to be living in Kingsport, Tennessee, but I also wanted to be married in my hometown of Spartanburg, South Carolina, and in my home church, Bethel United Methodist.

I had accepted a job in Kingsport and rented an apartment for the year of our engagement. This was before the Internet and email correspondence, so I was most appreciative that my mother handled the details. Our wedding was everything I had ever imagined.

Many, many times during the planning of our daughter's wedding, I thought of my mother and wanted to call her to tell her about what I was planning or ask her a flower question, because I knew she would know.

Then, I would pause with another silent prayer of thanks to God for giving me such a fine and outstanding mother.

When my husband and I were married, a male soloist and friend of our family from church sang "The Lord's Prayer," and it was unbelievable. To this day, people still talk about his beautiful voice, and he still sings in the choir.

At Mama's funeral, he sang the hymn again with every bit of the emotion expressed at our wedding. Our daughter wanted a man to also sing this at her wedding.

When the time arrived to plan the music, many worried. Our dear friend and church organist was going to be out of town on December 28th, the date of the wedding. Her children live in Texas, and traditionally, she would always leave on Christmas Day, following Christmas Eve services, to be with them.

Of course, God tells us not to worry. In 1 Peter 5:7 we're told, "Cast all your anxiety on him because he cares for you."

Our organist was not worried, and neither was I. In fact, she knew just the right musicians to step-in and offer exactly what we wanted for the traditional, seasonal wedding.

As fate would have it, the very same thing had happened when my mother and father-in-law celebrated their 50th wedding anniversary. Our organist had been scheduled to play, but she had to go out of town.

Her backup person did a fabulous job on the piano for the anniversary celebration, and he and his lovely wife were the pianist and organist for the wedding. The male soloist that was enlisted also shares a connection to my in-laws and lives in the house they built and lived in when Brad and I began dating.

Although he was suffering from laryngitis the night of the wedding, his powerful voice sounded out "The Lord's Prayer," just as our soloist had done in South Carolina nearly 30 years ago. His performance of "Ave Maria" brought me to tears.

Everything was most reverent, and to this day, we still hear compliments about the beautiful music.

No one was more excited about attending the wedding than my adult reading student, Ralph. In fact, once Ralph found out our daughter was engaged, he asked about the wedding for months.

He had met her fiancé and was actually somewhat leery of him. Of course, we brushed it off as his being guarded toward our daughter, and it probably was just that. However, Ralph is very perceptive, and because of his host of disabilities, he may have intuitively picked up on something we all missed.

Regardless, he gave his blessing and was thrilled to know he would be sitting with the family. Our only hurdle was the reception. We knew it would be out of his comfort zone, so some sweet Sunday school friends agreed to take Ralph home after the ceremony.

The night of the wedding, he arrived in his "Sunday best" attire. For Ralph, even though it might be tight, colored jeans and dark tennis shoes, it always includes a tie.

Because of our family's connection to Clemson, Ralph donned all of his brand new Clemson apparel we had given him for Christmas, and he looked handsome.

Although the formal dresses were a little more revealing than Ralph was comfortable being around, he did pose for a photo with the bride. It is one of our favorite pictures from the wedding. In it, Ralph is bowed and kissing the bride's extended hand. The photo is reminiscent of Disney's *Beauty and the Beast*.

Matrimony Memories

In 2014, my husband, Brad, and I celebrated our 30th wedding anniversary. It really does not seem that long ago that my daddy walked me down the aisle of Bethel United Methodist Church, the church I grew up in and attended in Spartanburg, South Carolina. Generations of Whitlocks have gone to Bethel and have gotten married there—including my parents.

Photos capture the love of many wedding special moments. For this reason, we shared framed photos of generations of loved ones on both sides of the bride and groom's families at the wedding reception. Clustered together on a small table, these memories offered hope and promise.

One of my favorite wedding photos is one in which my mother and I are looking in the mirror together in our church parlor. We had the photographer take this photo because Mama also had the same picture, looking in the mirror on her wedding day in the same church with her mother, my grandmother, captured in her wedding album.

Even though both of these ladies have passed away, and our daughter's wedding was in a different Methodist church in a different city, we continued the tradition and had the same photograph taken in our church parlor as we looked in the mirror together.

The mother-daughter mirrored image is a reflection of unconditional love. In fact, all of our family photographs from that day mirror this love, and on Mother's Day, when all of the newly married brides were posting photos from their own weddings with their mothers, my daughter posted ours. She may not have been a wife, but she most definitely had been a bride. Our love, portrayed in the photo, was just as sincere and genuine that day as it is today.

I was as proud of my daughter, if not more, than any other past, present or future mothers of the bride, and this cannot be changed.

Father-Daughter Day

So many emotions are shared between families during weddings—especially the father-daughter interaction. From the day she learns about the Christian marriage ritual and becoming a bride, a young woman looks forward to the walk down the aisle on the arm of her father.

If a daughter is close to her father, she cherishes the semblance of blessing and leaving her parental home to form a new one with her husband. Our daughter was no different.

Prior to the wedding, the two had a special moment together in our beautiful church parlor. Alone, they talked, cried and shared a sentimental letter. The photographer had slipped in to capture the special moment, which is forever preserved in photos.

Knowing her father would not be alive for the cherished moment, another young girl we know with an ailing, aging father also captured the moment during what has become known as the father-daughter- walk.

At 67, her father had been diagnosed with stage-four cancer. Given only months to live, with or without treatment, following radiation, he opted for quality of life verse quantity.

Every little girl dreams her father will one day walk her down the aisle as a bride. However, knowing her father's diagnosis and ultimate prognosis, she knew this would not be the case for her.

However, she remembered reading about a young girl's wish to still capture the love and emotion a father-daughter share on a wedding day and somehow emulate this through the father-daughter-walk. Modeled after the similar situation, which appeared in the *Huffington Post* and went viral on the Internet, the 20-year-old young woman knew the father-daughter-walk was something she desired to do with her father.

With the help of hospice, family members and other selfless volunteers, the magic has been forever captured with memories she hopes to one day incorporate in her actual wedding.

Dressed in a long, white, flowing dress, the photos that would have normally been taken on her wedding day were made with her father. Although she knows he will not be able to be with her, memories from their very special father-daughter-walk, during which her attendants wore pink, her favorite color, and she exchanged sentimental notes with her father, will warm her heart from their special day forward. She also believes, one day, her father will be smiling in heaven on his only daughter when that special day does arrive.

For our daughter, the two did share the actual moment in our church, and they experienced as much love and emotion as any bride might exchange with her father. As they entered the sanctuary, and he walked his only daughter down the aisle of our church, Brad proudly scanned the crowd of friends and relatives who had gathered for the long-awaited, treasured moment. This, too, was a blessing, and it has also been captured in our treasured photos.

A Wedding Did Occur

Ecclesiastes 3:4
"a time to weep and a time to laugh, a time to mourn and a time to dance."

Immediately following the wedding, notes of thanks and congratulations arrived with various sentiments.

"What a pleasure it was to attend such a GRAND and I mean GRAND celebration at Allandale! Everyone was dressed in winter elegance...first class food, flowers and music. A night no one will forget! Once you get the pictures back, you will spend hours reliving the event."

Keep enjoying your "time to laugh and your time to dance," Ecclesiastes 3:4

As tradition would have it, plans were made in advance for her wedding portrait to be published in the paper on Sunday following the Saturday wedding. And, hers was.

We were certainly excited and anxious to share our joy. Even our senior pastor, who had performed the marriage, commented on hitting the mark with tradition on this, too.

Regardless of the eventual outcome and the short-lived marriage, a wedding happened. All of the love, joy and planning that goes into any wedding occurred, and it has been so difficult not being able to truly enjoy and share the beautiful photos, the video of the ceremony and reception, stories and even cherished memories.

In many ways, this has been like a death. We have all experienced a loss—especially our daughter. Yet, just as a person yearns to talk about a departed relative, we, too, wish to talk about the wedding. It's not like it didn't happen or it needs to be shoved under the rug. It did happen, and it was filled with love...our love for our friends and family.

The wedding program reflects the celebration of family. Each and every first cousin, all 11, is listed as an usher or program attendant, and their names were included in the newspaper. This was very important.

With a large family, it's often difficult to get everyone together. Some guests may not have appreciated a wedding during the holidays. For us, it was perfect. And aren't the holidays about being with family? What better time to celebrate the beginning of a new one?

A Family Affair

When my mother was living and our children were little, my three brothers and their families would enjoy annual beach trips to the Lowcountry of South Carolina. We would stay in a large house and spend a week making memories together as a family.

We spent days on the beach and evenings eating dinner together. Each of us would take turns being responsible for a night's meal. In an effort to make things easier, we finally talked Mama into letting us do this. However, she always found a way to still make numerous trips to the local Piggy Wiggly grocery store.

Not one for the sun, this was her way of still being "mama" of the brood. As a thank you, one year, we all signed a koozie from the Piggly Wiggly with notes to "Me," which was her name from the grandchildren. I still have that red koozie in a cabinet in our home.

Music always filled the house, and Whitlock family beach vacations included dancing and entertainment. Evenings were highlighted with talent shows by the grandchildren, which were followed by hours of dancing in the den and singing until the night's end.

Weddings have also been fun-filled celebrations for us. The receptions following the ceremonies have been a time to sing and dance together.

Our daughter's wedding reception was no different. The large tent on the grounds of Allandale had a clear ceiling that reflected the light from two chandeliers. From the road, it looked like a holiday postcard. The soft glow of candles and the glitter of Christmas balls in silver and gold reflected signs of the season amidst sprays of fir and magnolia on the tables.

As the band belted out the radio version of "Brown Eyed Girl," our daughter and her daddy stole the floor with an unrehearsed shag as they danced their father-daughter dance.

She would later learn this made her husband mad. Mad?

Her husband could not even pick a song for their dance together or the one with his mother. In fact, he did not care for any of the possible song selections. The band even offered to learn one, but he did not have a favorite to even suggest.

On the other hand, "Brown Eyed Girl" had blared on a cassette tape over the years during the numerous drives to school. Our daughter and her daddy always knew this was "their song," and one day, it would be their father-daughter dance. It was.

Later in the evening, when the band announced the last song of the night, they also added, "This is by request, and it's the bride's favorite."

Amidst streams of white Flutter Fetti, little did we know that Journey's "Don't Stop Believin'" would be so prophetic. What has always been a favorite Whitlock family song, years before it was used by the White Sox baseball team or reprised on the television program *Glee*, would also become her mantra.

As the beginning of that all-too-familiar tune filled the tent of remaining revelers, our immediate family joined the band onstage. Known to sing with conviction, whether the lyrics are correct or not, she and I did our rendition of a mother-daughter performance that was also unrehearsed and unrivaled. Cheers from brothers, uncles, aunts and cousins spurred us on as we ended the celebration with the night's final song.

Not wanting to totally take over the stage, we looked for the groom and had him join on the last verse. Reluctant to be back onstage, he did rejoin his bride before their departure.

Brad and I were the last to leave. The band had packed up, all of the guests had gone and rain now poured down on the tent. The two of us sat down in chairs and reflected on the night. We had no idea what lay ahead.

The Right Thing

In the weeks following the wedding, our daughter immersed herself in getting their household together. During the day she busied herself with her classroom, and during the evening, she wrote thank you notes. Most of the time, her husband was at work, but she passed it off as being consumed by his new job position.

Occasionally, he would comment on the fact that the wedding was over and wondered why she was still preoccupied with it. Of course, she said there were lots of people who needed to be thanked, and she was writing thank you notes for them and keeping track of gifts.

Despite his wish to annul the marriage, she felt it was only nerves. Eventually, he would settle in, and they would develop a routine. For her, it was necessary to move forward, and thanking guests for their gifts was top on her list.

Since the children were little, we always insisted they learn and practice writing thank you notes. From the time they were able to craft sentences, both of our children learned the importance of being thankful and following the receipt of a gift with a personal, handwritten note.

Although a bride is allowed ample time for this gesture, our daughter felt this needed prompt attention despite their marital situation.

In fact, one evening, he arrived home to find her busy with the gift list and writing thank you notes well into the evening.

Disturbed, he asked why she was doing it. She replied with, "Why wouldn't I?" He just shrugged and mumbled that he just would not do it.

With each note, she relived the heartache as she hoped and prayed the situation would be resolved.

The Aftermath

2 Timothy 1:12

*"That is why I am suffering as I am. Yet this is no cause for shame,
because I know whom I have believed, and am convinced that he is able
to guard what I have entrusted to him until that day."*

She had taken a covenant and promised "for better or for worse."
Surely, this was "the worse." Regardless, she knew to trust in
God and have faith.

Newly married friends, who had fulfilled their expected destinies, could not understand her situation. Should she have known?

Walking down the aisle and looking at her father, rather than
her soon-to-be husband, should have been a sign. Instead of looking
anxiously ahead to her future, she was clinging to the one man who
truly had her respect.

It would be hard for any man to measure up to her father. Plus,
since she had already endured one broken engagement, what would
people think of her if she called it off?

Her husband was a much weaker man, but he did respect her
dad. In her mind, this combination would work well. Her father and
brother would still have their relationship. They would continue
to hunt and do outdoor activities without feeling like they had to
include him.

Although more of a "hacker" than a golfer, her husband did know how to play the game, and they could invite him to the links. He also loved Clemson and enjoyed tailgating and going to the games with the family. He had even made a road trip in the family RV to an away game with the male relatives.

More of a guest than a participant, who would help with the normal camping and tailgating details, he did purchase premium entrance tickets to get my daughter's brother and a friend into a club so that they would not have to wait in a long line for approved entrance. Once inside, he also disappeared, and although they repeatedly sent him text messages, he never responded and had to make his own way back to the camper.

Should this have been a sign? It probably should have been, but in the midst of celebration, people are given the benefit of the doubt, so the incident was dropped.

House

Settled in her dollhouse, which was exactly like the rental she had shared across the street, there was a sense of peace. It was hers. She had always done the right thing and saved her money. It was rewarding to purchase something all her own.

As an engaged couple, the two had decided to live in her house once they were married. Their neighbors had done the same, and they could make the small home work for a few years and save money.

His house sold fairly quickly, and many things were put in storage. Even though they had initially looked for a house to buy together, they were not able to find one.

She decided to paint, redecorate and begin making her home theirs. The dollhouse, with its vibrant colors, was converted into a more demure setting, with his choice of colors, for the two of them. She had even moved her couch out, anticipating that he would bring his, but in February, she was still waiting.

He was not bothered and would lie on the floor to watch television rather than moving his couch into their home. Later, we would all learn this was because he had another place, an apartment he could use as an escape.

***

Homes serve as our refuge and are sanctuaries for most. However, when life takes a dramatic turn, it is often best to relocate or redecorate. I have experienced both.

After my mother passed away, over 10 years ago in the sunroom of our family home, my daddy chose to stay in the home. Today, it still looks the very same way as it had when Mama was alive.

Aside from a new refrigerator, which was a necessity, the home has remained a shrine to her memory. In some way, it must be very comforting, because I can sense her presence when I am there. Yet, it must also be haunting. I look around every corner and in every room thinking I will see her. Echoes of voices and laughter from the past cause us to replay scenes from days spent there together.

When her brand-new husband first uttered the word "annulment" during their honeymoon, our daughter actually thought he was kidding. Who wouldn't?

When the wedding was being planned, he had shown little interest in the details. In fact, he referred to wedding planning as a "woman's sport."

In her mind, he was just nervous about the new responsibilities. He had been single for years, and married life meant changes.

However, after months of enduring his absences and being ignored when he was home, it was becoming clear that something was wrong.

Awakening one morning and readying for school, she casually mentioned possibly needing help with the mortgage. Even though she could afford it, there had been an unexpected expense, a new heat pump, that month, which she had covered.

He did not respond to the statement nor to her question regarding help, so she asked again.

Begrudgingly, he replied, "I cannot help with the mortgage when I pay rent."

Of course, she laughed continued dressing and replied, "You do not pay rent. We're married."

He said, "And, I have an apartment."

New Beginnings

Hebrews 11:1
*"Now faith is confidence in what we hope for
and assurance about what we do not see."*

Easter symbolizes rebirth and new beginnings, so during the Easter season, we decided it was time to tell our family members about the marriage. The Bible tells us God hates divorce. However, He does not hate His children.

Annulment, separation and divorce wreak havoc on families and society. Many are hurt in its wake. God knows this, and when He hates something, it is because He does not want us to hurt and others to suffer.

We knew it would be difficult to articulate what had transpired. We wanted each to personally hear the devastating news of the dissolved marriage from us or our daughter, but we knew this would be impossible.

So my husband crafted a letter, which was shared with close friends and family members. This was circulated right after Easter.

We also knew it would be difficult to attend church together with our daughter at First Broad Street United Methodist Church for the first time since the wedding. That Easter, we escaped to Daufuskie Island and attended church on Easter Sunday at First Union African Baptist Church.

A nondenominational, community church, the First Union African Church dates back to the 1880s and is the oldest building on the island. The original church, which was established in 1881, burned. The new church was reconstructed in 1884.

Because Jesus suffered, died and arose from the dead so our sins could be forgiven, we continue our life journeys as we become perfected through our trials and tribulations so that one day we may also rise and live in eternity.

"Jesus said to her, 'I am the resurrection and the life. The one who believes in me will live, even though they die;'" John 11:25

Like the waves of the ocean washing the shore anew, our family felt revitalized and renewed as we worshipped together on that Easter morning.

Circle of Life

Romans 5: 3-4
"Not only so, but we also rejoice in our sufferings,
because we know that suffering produces perseverance;
perseverance, character; and character, hope."

As a writer, I am possibly more attuned to foreshadowing and symbolism than most. However, if we just look around our everyday lives, we can see many signs of it.

Ironically, the last time we were on Daufuskie Island with our daughter's intended, they were actually installing a fire alarm in the villa. What was normally a tranquil porch setting became an erratic morning of hammering, banging and testing of the new, blaring alarm for emergencies. Little did we know we were living one.

May through October is nesting season for sea turtles. During our visits to Daufuskie Island, we walk the beach of the barrier island in search of signs of loggerhead sea turtles.

I had always been fascinated by the fact that the mother turtle returns to or near her birth beach and had read all about this in detail in *New York Times* bestselling author Mary Alice Monroe's novel *The Beach House* and her children's book *Turtle Summer*.

In fact, as I detailed in my first adult Christian book *Reading with Ralph–A Journey in Christian Compassion*, following my "coincidental" reading of *The Beach House*, God connected me to Mary Alice Monroe, and she is now my friend and a mentor.

Monroe beautifully parallels life with nature, and because I had read all about the sea turtles, I knew the importance of the hatchling imprinting on the sand of the beach and not picking up the small turtles no matter how much you might want to help them make it to the ocean.

Isn't this a lot like our very own life journeys and how our Heavenly Father must feel about us, His children? Even as He sees us struggle with hardships and adversities, Gods knows the outcome, and He uses various trials to mold and make us stronger in preparing us for our destinies and for our eventual eternal lives with Him.

During adversity, God gives us strength. Only He can completely change our perceived destiny to use life situations for His ultimate glory. I believe that is exactly what happened with the wedding and this little book.

When nest number three "boiled" on Daufuskie Island in August 2013, we were not there to see a concave indention in the sand, which indicates activity, and 48 of the inventoried hatchlings pile out of their bed on top of one another like boiling water to make their little way to the beach. However, a few days later, we were there to see one of the two remaining stragglers emerge from the nest and make its way out and into the ocean.

The experience could not have been more prophetic. With every climb the tiny turtle made, it would almost reach the top of the hole only to fall right back down on its back and have to start all over again and again.

As we watched the struggle, our adult children begged for me to just help it out of the hole. Even our young Labrador, Fuskie, who is named for the island, barked as if to cheer on the little warrior.

With every try and every fall, I could tell the turtle was getting stronger, and I knew this must, in fact, be a very real example of how God sees each of us, His children, in our lives.

Finally, with renewed strength and sand filled eyes, the hatchling did emerge from the protection of the nest and began making tiny tracks as it imprinted on the sand on its way to the ocean. If it survives the many perils of the sea, this same turtle may, one day, come ashore on this very same beach to lay eggs of its own in about 30 years.

Turtle Team

Once Bradley moved to Daufuskie Island, he became part of the island turtle team. The volunteer venture takes dedication and determination, and not too many young men would get up before sunrise to comb the beach for turtle tracks, possibly relocate nests above the tide line, as well as mark and monitor others.

However, this interest began when he was a young boy and had first learned about the effort to save the sea turtles. In elementary school, Bradley even did a report on the sea turtles. I love that our son is involved with something he is learning even more about, helping the island and educating others.

For any turtle team volunteer, the effort is daunting. Yet, the reward comes in caring about the connectedness turtles provide to the beaches and knowing you are helping sustain this. It's important these creatures continue coming ashore to nest. Each egg and hatchling provides much needed nutrients for our coastlines.

At the beginning of the season, we were thrilled to join him on his Saturday morning turtle duty. In the early light of predawn, a lamp shone in the living room facing the ocean. Bradley walked out of his room, with our faithful Lab in tow, crossing the villa to our room to awaken us for duty.

Knowing if we were on time, we were late in his book, his sister and I were dressed and waiting on the screened-in porch. We watched his every move with a sense of pride we were ready and an even greater one for what he was doing.

"Did you wonder where we were?" asked my daughter as he came on the porch.

"Kind of," he replied. "But, this is like Christmas for Mama. I knew she would be ready!"

As we loaded up in the golf cart and made our way over to the turtle team leader's home to secure the rescue vehicle, the coolness of the morning hit our faces, and anticipation filled the air. Over time, it may become routine, but the excitement of discovering a nest never gets old.

Once the unmistakable "tractor looking" tracks coming out of the ocean have been identified, volunteers assess the area, looking for signs of the body pit.

Although they can discover what is known as a "false crawl," where the female does come ashore but decides not to lay, usually, tracks indicate a nest. If a nest is located below the tide line, volunteers have to find the eggs, then relocate, mark and number the nest.

During training, volunteers learn how to probe for eggs. Sea turtles can deposit over 100 eggs, and the hole has been described as the shape of an inverted light bulb. For practice, our son learned how to probe for eggs with buried hen eggs. Volunteers probe the sand for the "air pocket," which typically indicates a nest.

On this particular morning, he saw the tracks first, but he gave me the satisfaction of thinking I discovered them. It was exciting!

The process takes persistence. Bradley once dug over two feet down and as much across before finally locating the eggs.

On this day, we were nearly as frustrated when I began to probe some more and finally hit the air pocket. There were 157 eggs in this loggerhead sea turtle's nest, and they looked like a bee honeycomb stacked in the sand. One is always saved, and we would take this egg back to be stored in the vial, which will be sent off for DNA testing, tracking and evaluation.

As we put on gloves and secured the bucket for collecting the eggs that would be relocated, I lifted up a prayer of thanks to God. It was a blessing to be in nature, with my adult children, and doing this together.

Thank you, God.

Prayer Corner

Luke 5:16

"But Jesus often withdrew to lonely places and prayed."

Prayer is vital and the most important aspect in our relationship with God. Although it should be reverent, it does not have to necessarily be formal.

First and foremost, God deserves a relationship with us, His children, and I believe prayer can be a conversation. God just wants a relationship. He already knows our needs and desires, but He would also like to hear from us.

We said prayers at the wedding, and these were delivered both during the ceremony and before it. I led the encircled group of women, and our senior pastor said one with the men. My prayer had not been prepared in advance. It just poured out as thanks to God for the blessing of marriage and for being with us on that day. He most certainly was and always is with each of us.

Psalm 46:1 "God is our refuge and strength, an ever-present help in trouble."

I enjoy walking our Labrador. Most evenings, we venture out on a regular path in our neighborhood. Because we live in the mountains of East Tennessee, we have plenty of hills to traverse and seasonal, scenic vistas.

One of my favorite spots is midway through the walk on a quiet, circular street, which has little to no traffic. For me, the bend of the road is better known as "the prayer corner," and I have referred to it as this for years.

During my walks, I have sent many prayers of healing and thanksgiving and have had numerous talks with God. Surely, He laughs at what I feel is right for my life and smiles when, occasionally, I recognize His much better plan.

Of course, I have always prayed for our children's future mates. Even with our daughter, we believe the wedding had to occur.

If her fiancé could not, for whatever reason, call off the wedding, it had to happen. Only she could have ended the engagement. As her parents, we could not have made this decision for her.

If we had insisted they not marry, she would have always wondered if she had missed out on the love of her life and resented us for keeping her from him.

In fact, early in their courtship, we did question his age. He was nine years older and had never been married. For a short while, she quit seeing him and dated a few others.

Yet, she always seemed to talk about him and mention his name. Finally, I asked if she loved him, and she admitted that she did. With this admission, we talked to her dad, and they began seeing each other again and dated three years before becoming engaged.

As the impending date of the marriage approached, she knew he was scared, but he had acted this way over any major life decision. Now, he was facing three—advancing to a new job position, selling his house and becoming engaged.

We noticed his change in personality the summer before the wedding, but we also dismissed it as his normal anxiety. Ironically, during the week this was most pronounced, we were all on Daufuskie Island together. Journal pages still reflect his presence, and our daughter wants them to remain. She attests it was a part of her life. Monogrammed beach towels, personally fashioned by her grandmother, also commemorate the bachelorette event, which took place on the island. Again, it was part of her history.

People ask if we feel differently about the island now or if we have any reservations about Allandale Mansion, which was where the wedding reception was held. Of course, we do not! This would be like asking if we could ever walk back in our church again because the wedding was there. Again, it was our church.

We gave our daughter her wedding. It was not trendy, nor did it reflect the latest fad in magazines or on television. Rather, her wedding was what she had always wanted and reflective of years of hopes and dreams. Through faith, those are still alive today.

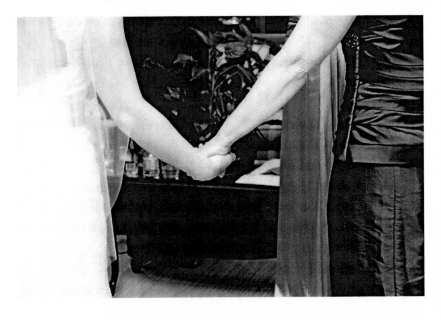

God in Dog

Revelation 5:13
"Then I heard every creature in heaven and on earth and under
the earth and on the sea, and all that is in them, saying:
'To him who sits on the throne and to the Lamb be
praise and honor and glory and power, for ever and ever!'"

Anyone who has ever loved a dog will admit its unconditional love is unparalleled on earth except for the love of God. For this reason, there is probably no coincidence that dog spelled backwards is, in fact, God.

I first learned about this when some friends taught our Sunday school class. Their dog even made a guest appearance, and the class loved it. The letter reversal and the symbolism for love has also stayed with me.

The only bad thing about loving an animal, especially a dog, is having to say "goodbye," and inevitably, it happens to all dog owners.

If you are lucky enough to be blessed by the love of a dog in your life, the blessings of the unconditional love you receive in return will eventually live in your heart after the hurt of losing one heals.

***

Jewel was the biggest female in the litter, and she was definitely the alpha. When the children saw her swimming in a huge tin tub in the backyard, they fell in love and wanted to bring her home that very day. However, the female was spoken for and not for sale.

My husband still inquired, and the owner agreed to let her become our dog. And she was. Oh, Jewel certainly was our dog.

As Brad carried the puppy, which was draped over his arm, to the car, I could have never envisioned the dog she would become nor the amount of love she would bring to our family. Dogs capture our hearts with a love that is unrivaled and is the closest to God's unconditional love for us.

***

That Friday afternoon was a beautiful, spring-like day that beckoned our Lab to venture out of our yard. When our son realized that his beloved best friend, Jewel, had left the yard, panic set in, and an all-out search effort ensued.

She was "Lassie" for the children, and everyone in the neighborhood knew Jewel. Neighbors, with leashes in tow, set out in cars and trucks in search of our dog. Because it was already late afternoon, darkness soon ended our efforts, which had been to no avail. The worst scenarios began to permeate our thoughts. Jewel had just been bathed and was not wearing her collar. How would we ever get her back? Many prayers were said, and tears were shed.

A long stormy night drifted into the wee hours before daybreak, the time when duck hunters are used to being awake, and mine were. Our son was up with his dad discussing the next strategy for the search.

We began to form an assembly line, as some made signs for the neighborhood, and others placed calls to the area veterinarian hospitals. Friends and neighbors continued the search again, scanning the riverbanks by boat and scouring the neighborhoods by car. One friend visited the Humane Society, yet our Lab was not there.

Once the signs were posted, calls began to come in from people who said they had seen her. Encouraging "hurries" were expressed as each caller described a black Lab they had just seen. Our Suburban clocked over 170 miles that dreary Saturday during the unending search.

Finding it easier to remain in the vehicle, and certainly more comforting as it made us feel productive, we continued to drive while our home became "central dispatch" as our daughter manned the phone and fielded the leads to us in the vehicle.

Finally, as the day began to wane, <u>the</u> call came. Our daughter emotionally reported that a lady had called who might have Jewel. She had seen her on Friday night darting in and out of the traffic on the major highway near Allandale Mansion in our hometown of Kingsport, Tennessee. This lady worked for a local vet and knew that the dog must be someone's pet.

Upon calling this angel, we learned that this was, in fact, our dog she had rescued. She had found shelter for Jewel at the home of her mother, who was blind and had previously owned two, black Labs as guide dogs. She and her husband had fed and loved our dog that stormy night.

After noticing our signs the next afternoon on her way home from work, her mother said to go ahead and call the family, as she knew that they were missing their dog. Joyfully, we were reunited with Jewel, and the family was rewarded for their deed.

As we sat in our den that evening, Jewel sound asleep on her dog nest, a call came in from the angel, who explained that she and her mother had talked and had decided some of the reward was going to be given to the rescue fund at the veterinarian clinic for rescued pets in need of medical attention.

Goodness can come out of adversity, and my family was blessed with friends and neighbors who helped to locate our "Jewel." We are fortunate and proud to live in such a caring community.

As Jewel began to age, we discussed bringing in another Lab, and that's when we adopted Buoy. She was several months old and the timid runt of the litter, but Buoy was loving, and she adapted well to our family and the alpha, Jewel.

Together, the two were nearly inseparable, and she was a true "buoy" to Jewel in her latter years.

On what turned out to be Jewel's last Christmas with our family, Brad had a special surprise for us. We had been reading Josh Grogan's book *Marley and Me* aloud around the same time that the movie, starring Owen Wilson and Jennifer Anniston, had been released for the holidays. He purchased our tickets in advance and put them with the children's stockings.

The night we went to the theater together as a family, we barely survived the movie. As we exited, slipping out a side door in the front of the theater versus going back out into the mall, my whole family was sobbing and had very swollen eyes.

Although we had read the book and knew the outcome, it made what we were experiencing with Jewel a reality. Our beloved Lab was in the final months of her life, and we, too, would be experiencing loss.

The morning we knew was her last, I was awakened to Brad crying.

"What's wrong?" I implored.

"It's Jewel," he answered as he bent over and shuddered, overpowered by tears. "I can't get her up."

My husband is a strong, tough man with a very loving, caring heart. Jewel was his dog, and he knew it was time. She was over 14 years old, and this was old for a Lab.

I drove the Suburban to the vet with our dog and two grown men, my husband and our son, holding her in the back and giving Jewel all she wanted of her favorite "pig-in-a-blanket" treats.

Jewel was a very large Lab, so the vet came out to our vehicle. Plus, she wanted to give us some privacy during our final moments together.

As the vet carefully shaved her paw before administering the heart-stopping drug, we said our goodbyes together, holding onto our beloved pet.

We enter this life alone, and we leave it alone. When Jewel took her final breath before lapsing into an eternal sleep, a lone Canada goose flew overhead in the morning sky, honking out an all-too-familiar call and prophetically ending a legacy.

***

Over the next few years, Buoy and I became even closer. We continued our early evening walks together, and she even made several trips with us to Daufuskie Island.

On what ended up being her last trip, Brad and I both detected a noticeable difference in her. In fact, as we sat on the beach with our dog between us, Buoy seemed uncharacteristically stoic.

It was a windy afternoon, and she was content to sit right between us. With the sand clinging to her black coat, she simply stared out at the ocean as if she were pondering life. We joked that she resembled a true "salty dog." She must have known this was her final outing to the island.

I thought that Buoy would have about the same lifespan as Jewel. In spite of having a little, white "Santa Claus" beard, she seemed much younger. Just a couple of months later, I was shocked to learn she was in kidney failure at age 10.

We were buddies. The family called her my co-worker. As an empty nester, she was my "personal buoy," and I prayed about this. My constant thought was, God, *how can you take my dog–especially now when we have become so close?*

The same trip to the same vet was happening all over again too soon. Our family was together, but this time I was riding in the back of the SUV holding onto my dog's paw.

Just moments before, Bradley had taken Buoy to the Holston River one last time, and Brad had come home with her favorite treat, French-fries.

Instead of being given one or two, Buoy was allowed to plunge her head into the bag and eat all she wanted. The rest were positioned under her front leg when she joined her buddy, Jewel, and was buried on the hill.

Those two Labs were our "Old Dan and Little Ann" from the classic novel *Where the Red Fern Grows* by Wilson Rawls. We loved Jewel and Buoy, and they gave us the same unconditional love that we receive from our Heavenly Father.

We had talked about one day getting another Lab. In fact, if we ever got another, it was decided her name would be Daufuskie, and we would call her "Fuskie."

Not by coincidence, some friends who were known for their Lab puppies, were expecting a new litter at the end of the summer. Others who were on the waiting list heard about our loss of Buoy and decided we needed first pick of the black females.

When the puppies were allowed visitors, we could not wait to see them! Of course, all babies are precious—especially Labrador puppies.

It was fun just visiting the dogs and being around Labs again. When we picked up the females, one bonded with us by "holding on" with her front paw. We knew we had found our dog.

Each time we visited, that little paw grasped us and held on. Finally, the day arrived for her to come home and officially join our family.

Of course, we went through an adjustment period. It had been a long time since we had introduced a new puppy to our home.

During the first few weeks, I wondered what we had done. This little Lab had more energy than a toddler! In fact, I often called Fuskie the "devil dog!"

She would play on our screened-in-porch, hang from the tablecloth, teethe on the floor and door jam, and it became her mission to conquer anything within her reach. I was exhausted.

When we were finally able to walk around the block, our neighbors got a kick out of our leash training sessions. My new puppy was spinning herself around on the leash and looked more like a child's top toy than a dog.

Finally, as the weeks wore on, we adjusted. Fuskie learned about us, and we learned about her. Our third Labrador retriever was a true combination of the other two.

I never could have envisioned that this dog would become my best buddy, but she sure has. Just as our life hurdles bring us closer to God, everything we endured as Fuskie matured prepared us for the lasting, loving relationship we share today. How prophetic.

Storms

Proverbs 3: 5-6
"Trust in the LORD with all your heart and lean not on your
own understanding; in all your ways acknowledge him,
and he will make your paths straight."

When the night's winter drizzle began falling after the ceremony, and the heavens opened up to a downpour, it should
have been symbolic of what was ahead. Yet, some say it's good luck
for it to rain on your wedding. Right? Unfortunately, this was just
the beginning of the storm.

Only later would we learn even the owner and the driver of the
antique "getaway" car had detected something amiss between the
newlyweds as they left the reception from our city's historic Allandale
Mansion.

Over the years, I have realized that not everyone has true love. In
any relationship, there will always be ups and downs, and this message
is captured in the sacred vows.

Have you ever worked a puzzle and tried your very best to make a
piece fit? With true love, the puzzle of life comes together. It's assembled
piece by piece until God completes His full picture, and the entire
image is revealed. Like any puzzle, all of the pieces fit together, and they
are not forced.

If we could only be attuned to the work of the Holy Spirit in our lives, we would recognize God is at work making each piece of our "life puzzle" fit, and only He can complete it.

Because we have been given free will, we make choices, and sometimes they will be wrong. However, ultimately God works all things toward His ultimate good and for His glory for His children.

We are challenged to have faith and to trust Him. In true love, one would never think of leaving. You weather the storms in life—together.

In order for this to happen, both parties need to be totally committed and without any doubts. Obviously, he was wrestling with doubt.

God's Armor

Luke 21:15

"For I will give you words and wisdom that none of your adversaries will be able to resist or contradict."

Verses were posted on the bathroom mirror, and I smiled with pride knowing my niece was learning God's word. Even if she did not remember every word, they would stay with her and come forth when she needed them.

We were staying with my youngest brother and his family, and I was reminded of the importance of learning scripture. Whether it's in church, Sunday school or Bible study, if we hear scripture, it changes our lives and becomes part of our hearts.

Often, we only call on these lessons when we are sharing them with others or during times of need. It is during these times that we are also able to find comfort.

This happened to me early on in my work career. I was gathered in a room of co-workers and something came up about heaven. Someone asked how I knew it existed, and I replied with a Bible verse.

"All I know is ... 'I have prepared a place for you, and in my mansion I have many rooms. If this were not true, I would not have told you.'"

The room immediately became silent. Of course, the familiar verse I paraphrased is from the book of John.

John 14:2
"My Father's house has many rooms; if that were not so, would I have told you that I am going there to prepare a place for you?"

However, I am a Methodist and, unlike my Baptist friends, I had not memorized many Bible verses. Yet, when I needed the words, scripture was given to me. This had to be from the power of the Holy Spirit.

A similar incident happened one day when I was in my car listening to the radio. Ted Turner was saying something about the Bible being dated and in need of revision because it was not applicable to today's world.

Immediately, I began shouting at my radio.

"That's not true!" I yelled. "Jesus Christ is the same yesterday, today and forever."

Hebrews 13:8
"Jesus Christ is the same yesterday and today and forever."

Going Forward

Romans 8:28
"And we know that in all things God works for the good of those who love him, who have been called according to his purpose."

Humor helps us deal with the complexities of life, and when the title of this book came to me, we had visions of Kathryn Stockett's bestselling novel *The Help*. In the novel, which was also made into a movie, a member of the community becomes very concerned that a certain book, which had just been published, might portray her in a poor light.

Thinking this would ignite the very same fear in some, honestly, we laughed. Yet, that's as far as the humor went because, of course, I would never write in a way that portrayed anyone in a poor light. However, I will divulge the truth, and if this is harmful, I am not ashamed.

Our church recently finished a sermon series entitled "Faith Stories." Each of us has a story, and our ministers shared how we can use these stories of faith to share God with others. My hope is that this book might be a blessing that will shine God's light for others through our "faith story."

Our earthly lives will hold many trials and tribulations, yet even in times of difficulty, God is <u>always</u> with us on our journeys.

Isaiah 41:10
"So do not fear, for I am with you; do not be dismayed,
for I am your God. I will strengthen you and help you;
I will uphold you with my righteous right hand."

Remembering that God loves us, and He is with us, helps each of us in our life journeys. After the agony and the tears, there is always a "silver lining," and we are able to see God's blessings.

Most little girls do dream about a wedding, and they all hope for a happy ending. Regardless of the outcome, weddings hold blessings. Simple gifts like being together as a family and a father being able to walk his daughter down the aisle are blessings of the moment.

The blessings of music and the nuptial message from the pastor serve to minister to those in attendance. If a bond is renewed through hearing scripture and the covenant vows, or a heart is encouraged through song, the wedding has been a blessing, and our Heavenly Father has received all honor and glory.

Our daughter will move beyond this turmoil. God has written her story, our story, and He has also written yours. Only He knows every chapter and every remaining piece of the puzzle, and He will always be with us. For this reason, I trust Him with the next chapter and with the ending, too!

Thank you, God!

Amen

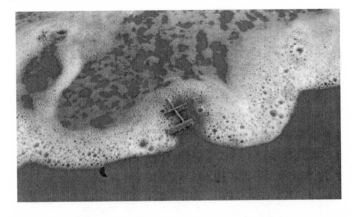

Afterword

Our family was blessed by sentiments from others about the breakup of the marriage. Some excerpts are shared below:

Notes from Others

There had been no hint that there was any problem at all within your family. It is almost more than I can take in. It has taken me these two days to know how to respond. First of all, it breaks my heart to think what all of you have been through. It is "pain" in the real sense of the word; and it is the kind that is truly felt. All of you are upset about the same thing but in four different ways. All of it is so very sad. Stress and trauma take a lot out of a person.

Now, I'm going to be brave and offer you some advice, only because I have experience in a situation similar to this... my "almost" first wedding.

We dated for six years without one single argument and no break-up. It never occurred to me to ever look at another man. It was the perfect love, or so I thought. Just before the wedding, I learned that he had been going out with another woman, and it just about killed me. He assured me all was okay, and he was certain we would be fine. On the day of the wedding, with a church full of people, me in my dress, the bridesmaids all set to go, a friend came to me in the room where I was waiting for the director to come get me. His message to me was that my intended was very sick and could not make it to the wedding. I had him sent to the hospital, where it was discovered by doctors that there was nothing wrong with him. And the story goes on. It did not take me long to realize that being "left at the altar" was the best thing that could possibly have happened to me.

Here is my advice: It is for certain that God has something and someone better for you. One of the most important things I can tell you (and all the family) is to ask the Lord to cause your feelings about him to be neutralized. Strange word. This is so there is no lingering love to deal with and NO hatred to hurt or harden your heart.

This too will pass, and in years to come, there will be no regrets. I promise.

***

My mind continues to reel over what has transpired, and I can make no sense of it whatsoever. I am overly analytical and seek reason in every situation, despite knowing that some of life's twists and turns simply cannot be explained. As such, I have been so impressed and encouraged by your daughter's resolve to trust, rather than give in to questioning, God's plan for her life and know that you have surely bolstered such resolve in the most difficult hours. Please know that I am but one of many who are thinking of and praying for you. For those of us who know and love you, this situation simply has no bearing on the wonderful person and family you are; we support you and look forward with you to brighter days ahead!

***

We have such admiration for you! What a great family you are and thank you for providing a wonderful role model for us all when we will face adversity, such as you have. Your daughter is a strong person and strong Christian thanks to her parents—just imagine what would be happening if she didn't have this backing and the love for each other you all have.

I found these two sentences in a devotion I wanted to share with you.

"When most of your mental energy goes into efforts to figure things out, you are unable to receive this glorious gift (peace). I look into your mind and see thoughts spinning round and round: going nowhere, accomplishing nothing. All the while, My Peace hovers over you, searching for a place to land."

Good words which we hope help. You are in our prayers.

"For I am the Lord, your God, who takes hold of your right hand and says to you, Do not fear; I will help you." Isaiah 41:13.

***

You are to be commended on the way in which you have chosen to make family and friends aware of the status change. I have the utmost respect for you. Not many parents would have stepped up to the plate to square it away with friends with such a noble letter.

May God continue to help ease the pain that has permeated your lives. He will continue to reveal to you His protection over your daughter. It will be interesting to see how God will use this devastating situation in your lives to glorify Him. Oh, yes, He will!!!!

***

Broken hearted for her. The best is yet to come. Sadly he was not the best. I will hold her in my prayers.

***

It's the troubling times like these that we do not stop having faith but begin to exercise our faith.

I do believe that God has a plan, and although it may not be "our" plan, we just have to hold faith that it's for the best. Her strong convictions will carry her through.

LEIGH ANNE W. HOOVER

is a native of South Carolina and a graduate of Clemson University. With a Bachelor of Arts degree in secondary education/English and a minor in general communications, Hoover has worked for over 30 years in the media. She has extensive writing and public relations experience in the region and has published articles encompassing personality and home profiles, arts and entertainment reviews, medical topics, and weekend escape pieces.

Notable features include one-on-one interviews with actress Andie MacDowell, artists Bob Timberlake and P. Buckley Moss, author Jan Karon, Grammy-winner, singer/songwriter Kenny Loggins and the 14th president of Clemson University, James F. Barker. Hoover also writes a monthly column for *East Tennessee Medical News* titled "Enjoying East Tennessee."

She is the author of the well-known children's book *The Santa Train Tradition* and award-winning *Festus and His Fun Fest Favorites*. Her children's books have been endorsed by *New York Times* bestselling author Mary Alice Monroe and parent educator Nancy Samalin.

Reading with Ralph—A Journey in Christian Compassion is a Christian book about her adult literacy student. *For Better or Worse...Unless Annulment Comes First* is Hoover's second adult Christian book.

Hoover serves as president of the Friends of Allandale board of directors and is a member of the Kingsport Delphian Club. She is also a past president of the Literacy Council of Kingsport, the Junior League of Kingsport and past co-chair of the Clemson University Parents' Development Board.

Hoover is a member of First Broad Street United Methodist Church, and she volunteers as an adult reading tutor. She and her husband, Brad, reside in Kingsport, and they have two adult children.

BOOKS ALSO BY
LEIGH ANNE W. HOOVER

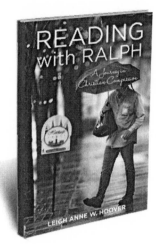

*Reading with Ralph–
A Journey in
Christian Compassion*

*Festus and His
Fun Fest Favorites*

The Santa Train Tradition

**Available at www.wordofmouthpress.us
www.thesantatraintradition.com
and from most major online booksellers**